Rehearse, Direct and Play

A Student's Guide to Group Music Making

William Lloyd and Paul Terry

shop@musonix.co.uk
trade distribution
online sales
0208 286 9947

• Musonix Publishing •

For Eugene Gomèche
in gratitude for countless hours of enjoyable music making
with the Chamber Music Competition for Schools

Other titles from Musonix Publishing:

Music in Sequence – A complete guide to MIDI sequencing
Classics in Sequence – A source book for MIDI sequencing
The Studio Musician's Jargonbuster –
        A glossary of music technology and recording

First published in 1993.   ISBN 0 9517214 3 7

Published by Musonix Publishing, 2 Avenue Gardens, London SW14 8BP

Exclusive distributors:

Music Sales Limited, 8/9 Frith Street, London W1V 5TZ
Music Sales Corporation, 257 Park Avenue South, New York NY 10010
Music Sales Pty. Ltd., 4th Floor, 72 Bathurst Street, Sydney NSW 2000

Order Number: MX 30053

British Library Cataloguing-in-Publication Data.
A catalogue record for this book is available from the British Library.

Cover design by Bob Linney
Photo-typeset by Musonix Typesetting
Printed and bound in England

Contents

Introduction

Musicians hate wasting time. Of course we can all think of countless occasions when we meant to practise, but instead spent hours half-watching TV or staring out of the window or dismantling the instrument – anything to avoid getting down to work. It happens all the time, but at least we know there's only one person to blame. What musicians really hate is someone else wasting their time for them.

How often have you sat in an orchestra fuming because the conductor doesn't have a clue what to say to make the music work better? How often have you felt like screaming at a drummer who still can't get round a simple fill which should have been practised at home before the first rehearsal? How often have you spent half the session waiting for the keyboard player to set up and find a plug for the amp before anyone else can do any playing?

All these irritations get in the way of productive music making and yet all could have been avoided by some simple preparation. Ensemble music, whether for a four-piece Rock & Roll band or a symphony orchestra of 80, is primarily about people and how they respond to each other. The purpose of this book is to help you plan an ensemble performance from beginning to end; what to play; how to set up the rehearsals; what to say and do to get the best out of the musicians as you rehearse. In this way everyone will approach the eventual performance with the feeling that the whole process has been enjoyable and worthwhile.

Chapter One

Selecting Repertoire

Standard ensembles

When planning an ensemble, obviously the first consideration is to decide what instruments or singers are needed. Certain generic formats have become much more popular than others, usually because they offer a wide pitch range and a blend of timbres in which no one is masked. Thus you will find much more music written for a group consisting of two violins, viola and cello than for, say, tenor sax, guitar, recorder and euphonium. Sometimes it will not be possible to find players to match exactly the original instrumentation of a piece that you want to perform: some notes on arranging music to suit a particular combination are given later in the chapter. Here, however, are some of the most common ensemble formats:

Standard R&R Band	Lead Guitar, Rhythm Guitar and/or Keyboard(s), Bass Guitar, Drums, Vocals
Jazz Combo	Trumpet/Sax/Trombone, Piano, Bass and Drums
Brass Quintet	2 Trumpets, Horn, Trombone, Tuba
Brass Quartet	Trumpet, Horn, Trombone, Tuba
Wind Quintet	Flute, Oboe, Clarinet, Horn, Bassoon
Woodwind Quartet	Flute, Oboe, Clarinet, Bassoon
String Quartet	2 Violins, Viola, Cello
String Trio	Violin, Viola, Cello
Piano Quintet	2 Violins, Viola, Cello, Piano
Piano Quartet	Violin, Viola, Cello, Piano
Piano Trio	Violin, Cello, Piano
Saxophone Quartet	Four Saxophones of various sizes
Recorder Consort	Three or more Recorders of various sizes
Vocal Ensemble	Soprano, Alto, Tenor, Bass voices (SATB) or combinations such as SSA and SAB
Baroque Trio Sonata	Two melody instruments and continuo of bass instrument plus keyboard
Baroque Solo Sonata	One melody instrument and continuo

Note that a Piano Quintet does not involve the use of five pianos – such music would rarely be performable except in a retailer's showroom. Similarly, descriptions such as Clarinet Quintet and Oboe Quartet refer to just one wind player with strings. Original music for two or more identical instruments (such as three flutes) is much less common, although there are many arrangements for such groups.

If you can assemble the players or singers for any of these standard groupings there will be no shortage of music to perform. However, composers often wrote for accomplished players, and you may well find that one or more of the individual parts is far beyond the capabilities of the person that you had in mind. If you want to find original music that will not overstretch your team, it is worth looking at pieces by Haydn and other early classical composers such as C P E Bach, where the bass and inner parts in particular are often not too demanding. Minuet and Trio and other central movements are especially useful. Also, many baroque sonatas offer keyboardists and cellists playable music while providing a more experienced violinist or wind player with something to get their teeth into.

For groups with less experience of playing together, the various collections of renaissance dance music by Susato and Praetorius are a treasure chest of short, attractive movements for three to five instruments. These often contrast short contrapuntal sections, giving musical interest in each part, with rhythmically straightforward passages which are simpler to put together.

In general, music written before about 1750 is easier to adapt for different instruments than later, more idiomatically conceived pieces. Composers of that time were less inclined to write with a specific instrument in mind – Handel's solo sonatas, opus 1, were published for flute, violin, recorder or oboe (evidence of both flexibility and an eye for potential sales). Similarly, the continuo part can use various combinations of chordal and bass instrument and not just the ubiquitous pairing of harpsichord and cello. This might give you the opportunity to include a bassoon, acoustic guitar or electric keyboard with good harpsichord or pipe organ sounds in the group.

Ensemble music is almost always supplied as a set of instrumental parts, each showing the music for just one instrument. Chamber works with piano will usually include a full score for the pianist, with the music for each instrument printed above the piano part:

Mozart: Piano Quartet in G minor, K.478 (Rondo: bars 52-55)

For most other pieces you will need to obtain a full score (a pocket-sized "miniature" score will do) so that you can see what is going on. If you are directing the ensemble as one of the players, some juggling between your part and the score will be necessary in rehearsals.

Choosing jazz or popular repertoire throws up a rather different problem, since the printed music is usually just a simple guide which the player can elaborate. Jazz arrangements for larger ensembles are sometimes available fully written out, but most jazz numbers are issued as a "lead sheet" giving only the main melody and chord structure (suggestions for creating a "head arrangement" from this type of shorthand notation are given in the chapter on jazz and pop):

Cohan: Give My Regards To Broadway (Chorus: bars 1-4)

Much popular music is put together during rehearsal and recording sessions and isn't written down at all unless commercial success justifies the production of sheet music. Then it is generally published as an arrangement (often simplified) for voice and piano, with chord symbols for guitarists. A good ear and knowledge of the recording will be needed if you want to reconstruct the precise scoring of the original song. More detailed versions of some songs have started to appear (such as the "Rock Scores" and "Off the Record" series) but separate parts for individual performers are not available, and will have to be copied out by hand if your players expect to use music.

Arrangements

Because of the scarcity of suitable original material for many ensemble line-ups, there are innumerable albums of arrangements of both classical and popular hit melodies. These are often presented as all-purpose packages for flexible sized groups of various instruments. Such usefulness is balanced by two potential disadvantages. Firstly, in an attempt to be commercial, individual parts are often technically easy, but inner and lower parts can be very dull – making practising and rehearsing the music extremely tedious for these players. Secondly, the end result is unlikely to sound much like the real thing – a fact which may disappoint your audience who are familiar with the original. However, if you fancy the idea of an arrangement of *Yesterday* for four recorders and glockenspiel, with an optional piano part for the teacher, you can be pretty sure someone will have published one.

An alternative to a published arrangement is to make your own adaptation of a piece to suit the resources available. For example, a clarinet may be used if you lack a horn player, although it won't be able to reproduce the distinctive timbre of that instrument. There may be obvious difficulties of translation – a flute cannot play a double stopped chord found in a violin part, for instance. If you are adapting string parts for wind instruments, remember that players will need space to breathe. Music may need transposing, including taking whole passages up or down by an octave to avoid weak parts of the register or notes out of range. Key signatures of more than one or two sharps, which are comfortable for string players, can cause problems for transposing instruments such as the B-flat clarinet and most brass. The reverse is also true – string players may find flat keys awkward.

Despite these problems, adaptations (particularly of earlier music) can work very well. If you want to adapt later music it is important to remember that it will almost certainly have been conceived with its specific instrumental timbres as an integral component. While, for example, the alto sax can certainly play much the same pitch range as a viola, it may prove to be far too loud for the delicate second violin part which might run alongside it. Considerations such as these should not deter you, however, from trying to make an arrangement of a work you especially like to suit the particular forces at your disposal. Provided that you keep in mind the new set of timbres and try to give every player some interesting music, it should be possible to make an imaginative and colourful new interpretation which will also spare the blushes of the original composer and his fans.

Whilst it is important to select music that will suit the abilities and instrumentation of your group, the really vital thing is that you choose something that you really want to work on. An exciting piece will generate its own enthusiasm and will motivate everyone to make an extra effort to get round the notes and put in the hours of rehearsal until it comes right. Players will surprise even themselves in finding that they can perform music that everyone thought would be too hard for them, simply because someone had confidence and asked them to try. If the choice is between playing safe with something easy or going for it with the Hendrix or the Beethoven, you will find that taking the risk almost always pays off in the end.

Obtaining the music

Once you have decided what to play, the next task is to find copies of the music. Schools and colleges don't always have large collections of ensemble music, but most will have access to a County Music Library, Rural Music School or similar source that can usually lend music for an extended period of time. Also remember that you can borrow music from public libraries. Only the central libraries of larger towns carry a wide-ranging stock, but all libraries can obtain almost any piece of music through the Inter-Library Loans Service. You will need exact details of the piece you require, and don't forget to ask if parts for individual players are available. There may be a small reservation charge for obtaining the material. Librarians are there to help you and will probably enjoy doing so at least as much as exacting fines for overdue books! They can also show you how to use the library's cataloguing system, the micro-fiche systems that list all books in print, and where to find useful reference sources such as *The New Grove Dictionary of Music and Musicians* which lists the complete works of all major composers, including the instruments required.

Another obvious source is the music retailer. Local music shops have space to stock only a small selection of items, but they will have copies of publishers' catalogues that they will be happy either to give you or let you browse through. In these, mainstream classical works for ensembles will generally appear under "chamber music". If there is a choice of versions available, it may be between an *Urtext* edition, which keeps as close as possible to what the composer originally wrote, without editorial additions such as bowings or phrasing, and a more interpretative version produced by a leading performer. Once you have found the item you want, the shop can order it and will usually be able to have it ready for you within a week or so.

For people who find it difficult to get to a music shop, most publishers can supply items from their catalogues direct by post. Some publishers will also hire material, particularly modern and rare works, although this can be expensive.

Much of the less mainstream repertoire is published by companies who specialize in music for a particular type of instrument – recorders or brass ensemble for instance. Instrument retailers may carry more information about such publications than a general music shop. One of the largest of the specialist suppliers is June Emerson[1], whose catalogues include thousands of pieces for woodwind and brass groups from many different publishers.

Pop music is published by a variety of small and large companies: ask at the music shop to see the catalogues of the main distributors, such as Music Sales and IMP, which collect these together in lists of music arranged by order of solo artist and group. Some of the best sources of lead sheets for jazz and pop are the collections known as "real books" and "fake books" (or "buskers' books") that provide just the outline melody, chords and lyrics of thousands of songs for a reasonable price.

Record catalogues are useful if you like the work of a particular group whose line-up matches your own – you may also glean information about any arrangements that they have recorded. Browsing through the racks of individual CDs in a record store is a good way to discover the timings of pieces.

The question of how much to play is vital when programme planning. If you are presenting a whole concert, remember how much extra stamina is required when playing in public – feeling exhausted by the interval will not help your concentration and commitment in the second half. Few people have ever been to a concert that they felt was too short – although the cynical use of support acts and merchandising commercials by some bands can leave an audience feeling both tired *and* ripped off. For ensemble playing which forms part of a public exam, check the syllabus about timings – generally no more than a few minutes of music is required. The golden rule here is to present polished, well thought-out performances and never to ramble on and on. Examiners, like audiences, hate wasting time too.

---

1   June Emerson, Windmill Farm, Ampleforth, North Yorkshire.

Checklist

◆ **Choose** music that
   suits the abilities of the ensemble and will interest and
   excite you, the players and your audience

◆ **Beware** of arrangements that
   may include boringly easy parts for some players or
   may not sound anything like the original version

◆ **Consider**
   what adaptations you might reasonably be able to make
   to tailor an existing piece to your requirements

◆ **Research**
   Public libraries and county music libraries
   Music retailers
   Specialist retailers and mail order suppliers
   Publishers' catalogues
   CD catalogues
   Reference sources such as *The New Grove*

◆ **Remember**
   that time spent finding the right music will avoid time
   wasted on problems later and will provide all concerned
   with material that is enjoyable to work on

Chapter Two

Preparing the Score and Parts

Checking the music

Unless your group intends to improvise its performance (and even then some predetermined guidelines will be needed), music on the stands at the first rehearsal will be essential if anything is to happen. In fact, it is much better to give the parts out well before this – not everyone is a good sight-reader and most will appreciate some time in which to take the music to their instrumental teacher and generally practise it in readiness. Keyboard players, who almost always have the most notes to play, will particularly require the music early. Inexperienced members of the group may need to be reminded at this point of the difference between:

♦ **practising** – which is done individually beforehand, and

♦ **rehearsal** – at which parts are expected to have been at least basically learnt, so that the group can immediately begin working on putting the piece together.

As director, you will need all the charm, persuasion and firmness you can muster to make sure this happens – prepared music will save hours of rehearsal time and frayed tempers later.

Before giving the parts out, check each one with the full score to make sure that there are no differences since mistakes are not as rare as you might expect. It may be sensible to have a spare copy of each part in case of loss – also not that rare! However, note that photocopying music is generally illegal. Even when the composer is long dead, modern editors and publishers retain a copyright in respect of the time and money they have invested in preparing and printing the music. An exception is made, however, to allow photocopying of a few bars needed to help a player negotiate an awkward page turn.

In rehearsal, the group will need to be able to locate places in the music that you may want them to start from. Many parts are issued with bar numbers printed every ten bars or at the beginning of each line. An alternative system uses "rehearsal letters" – capitals at the start of important sections in the music. Check that one or other of these methods is used in the parts and that the letters or bar numbers tally with those your full score (they may well not do so if the score is a different edition to the parts) so that when you say "let's go from two after A" the others know what you are talking about.

Vafadari: A Square Mile Smile (bars 20-23)

Bass Guitar

"Two after A" or Bar 23

Getting to know the score

Make sure that you understand the layout of the score. Check that you know where any repeat signs lead back to and how repeat directions such as *da capo* and *dal segno* work. Decide which repeats you want the group to observe and mark the parts accordingly. If a repeat leads back to the beginning, always practise this re-start, as the opening will feel different the second time round. Two types of repeat often cause problems. One is the use of alternative first- and second-time bars. Be ready for your preliminary run-through to fall apart at such places, with some players going back and others reading on from the first-time bar to the second-time bar, quite forgetting about the repeat. Also beware of repeat signs in the middle of bars:

Gavotte

Even if the players notice the repeat, many will be tempted to stop when faced with a double bar-line across the stave. Before you start rehearsing such a piece, remind players to practise making a totally seamless repeat back *(see right)*.

Look up any unfamiliar instructions or signs and have answers for awkward questions such as "how do you play those *staccato* notes where the dots have got a slur under them?" or "does a *crescendo* followed by *p* mean increase from *pp* to *p* or does it mean *crescendo* to loud and then play softly?". Knowing a little jargon can be useful – experienced players tend to refer to *crescendo* and *diminuendo* signs as "hairpins", to wedge accents as "hats" and to pause signs as "eyebrows", for example. It is also quicker to say "go from the *tutti*" rather than "start from the place where we all come in together".

In ensembles with strings, players may need to have some bowing instructions marked into the parts as it is often important for the bowing to be unanimous. If in doubt, ask a senior player or an instrumental teacher to help you with this.

Familiarity with technical terms used by various instruments is also helpful. This will save the embarrassment of yelling at a violinist for holding the bow upside down when the part is marked *col legno*. If you know the meaning of *con sordino* you will realize that it may be necessary to remind your string or brass players to bring their mutes.

String players, by the way, have an almost irrational hatred of calling a slide between notes a *glissando* (which they take to mean a very fast chromatic scale with audible semitones): they, like singers, call a slide *portamento*. However, trombonists, will look blank if you ask for *portamento* – they always say *glissando*, semitones or not.

As a rule, don't get too worried about these eccentric niceties – you can pick them up from players as you go along. However, one specialist area that may need your attention is the type of notation used for some instruments whose pitch range falls between the treble and bass clefs. The C clef is used both in viola parts written in the alto clef, and in high bassoon, cello and trombone parts written in the tenor clef. The staves below give a quick translation, but it is usually easiest just to remember that the C clef straddles the line for Middle C and then to work out the other notes by counting up or down from this:

Alto Clef

Tenor Clef

Treble and
Bass Clefs

Some instruments use transposed parts. Most straightforward are those that play at the extreme ends of the pitch range. Double bass music, for example, is written an octave higher than it really sounds, while parts for piccolo and descant recorder are written an octave lower than their sounding pitches. In both cases this is to avoid too much use of leger lines. The same applies to guitar music and to tenor parts in vocal music, neither of which fits comfortably onto just the treble or bass stave. Conventionally both are notated in the treble clef and their music sounds an octave lower than written. With all of these octave transpositions, a small figure 8 is sometimes attached below or above the treble clef to remind you – but you can't rely on this.

Slightly more complicated are instruments which are said to be "in" a certain key: clarinets and trumpets in B-flat, for example, and horns in F. For various reasons, both historical and for ease of fingering, the music for these instruments is not written in the key in which it actually sounds. As a rule-of-thumb, the "key" of the instrument indicates the note that will actually sound when the performer plays the note C. All of the other notes can be worked out from this:

You will see that sounding notes are, for almost all transposing instruments, lower than the written pitch. Some clarinet parts require a clarinet in A – you may need to re-transpose these, as many players will have only a clarinet in B-flat (better still, persuade your clarinettist to do it!). Be aware that, if this is necessary, the part may end up in some very difficult keys. Most full scores print the music for transposing instruments exactly as it is in the player's part. However, some (especially easy, all-purpose arrangements) show each stave at "concert pitch", i.e. as it actually sounds. Here you need to take care, since a trumpeter who is seeing (and playing) an A in bar 2 will not understand when you refer to the same note as the G printed in your full score.

Musical decisions

Get to know the sound of the piece as thoroughly as possible before the group first meets. Decide on key elements of its character that you want your performers to communicate: rhythmic drive, a relaxed and dreamy atmosphere, elegance of phrasing, clarity of individual lines, dramatic contrasts or subtle blends. If there is a recording, it may help to listen through it several times, concentrating on the part played by a different instrument each time.

The better you become at "selective" hearing, the more quickly you will be able to spot and put right problems that arise in rehearsal. Try to identify beforehand sections which may prove difficult for ensemble and thus will need careful rehearsing. There may also be places where one instrument has a very awkward passage although the rest of the ensemble is quite straightforward:

Haydn (arr.)

It will not be particularly helpful to the second violinist to concentrate fiercely on this section in the early stages – further individual practice may be more useful. Learn to identify such sections and spare someone unnecessary embarrassment, as an uncomfortable or nervous player will not perform well.

If you are also playing in the group, practise your own part while imagining what you will hear around you and look for sections where you could stop playing temporarily to listen to the others. Whether you are conducting, or directing as a player, mark in your music any places where you will need to give a visual indication – changes of time signature, pauses, cut-offs, and "leads" where a player comes in for the first time, or after a period of rests, and may need your help.

Practise finding the tempo that you want for the music. Often it is easier to remember this from a passage in the middle of the piece, particularly if the beginning has slow or very fast-moving note values. The director of a vocal ensemble is also expected to decide on the places where the singers may breathe – more on this in chapter five.

All these pre-rehearsal activities may seem rather dictatorial. Surely, you may say, the point of an ensemble is that it works democratically, with each member taking an equal share of the responsibility. Of course no-one is suggesting that you shouldn't consult before making decisions on matters of repertoire, etc. In rock groups, jazz combos and chamber music, especially where all the players are equally experienced, every performer will sometimes be acting as director and sometimes responding to the lead and suggestions of others. In larger and less experienced ensembles, however, someone is needed who can act as a decision maker on tempo, balance, intonation and all those other parameters that will be dealt with in later chapters. This is part of your rôle as director. Someone also has to get the music, organize rehearsal times and places and check that everyone can play their parts; you are best placed to do this too.

Checklist

◆ **Check** individual parts against the score for accuracy and to ensure that rehearsal letters/bar numbers match

◆ **Make sure** you understand the score, including the layout of repeats, any unusual signs or performing directions, and the notation of any parts for transposing instruments

◆ **Listen** to a recording of the piece. Use the score to follow one part at a time, as well as listening to the effect of the whole

◆ **Decide** on tempi, things you want to communicate in the music and passages that may prove difficult for the entire group or that may require special individual practice

◆ **Hand out music** well before the first rehearsal and ensure that everyone knows of the need to practise before rehearsing

Chapter Three

Leading and Conducting

One of the most important functions of the director is to co-ordinate the ensemble sound. Large groups, and less experienced ensembles, will often need someone to conduct who is unencumbered by the demands of also having to play an instrument. Smaller, more cohesive groups can generally be led from within, although an extra pair of ears is useful to check the balance from further back in the hall. Whether you are intending to play in the group or direct it from the front, certain points will invariably crop up. Try to prepare a strategy for leading the music before the first rehearsal.

The Player-Leader

Working without a conductor throws up the problem of how to start a section together (working with one sometimes does, too!). One player, not necessarily always the same one, will have to give a lead which indicates both the tempo and the exact moment that everyone is to start playing. Nothing sounds more amateur than a whispered "1, 2, 3, 4" immediately before the opening of a piece, particularly when, as sometimes happens, the music is actually in three time. Get everyone to practise leading the ensemble, either with a clear lifting of the bow arm, a gesture with the end of the instrument or by a simple nod of the head. Remember that at least *two* beats are needed for everyone to be able to pick up the tempo. It is often a great help to imagine that you are about to sing the music, with a breath in on the beat before you want everyone to start playing.

As director, you will also need to be clear whether music such as:

Bourrée   *Bach: Orchestral Suite No.3 in D*

is to be felt in four or two beats to the bar. A choice between indicating dotted crotchets or quavers may similarly be presented by slow music in compound time. Of course, giving clear leads is actually a two-way process and everyone else must be aware of whom to watch at a given point. Persuade players to write this information into their parts.

Another useful technique for the group to practise is moving off a pause *(fermata)*. Eye contact is again essential for this, so try an easy exercise that everyone can quickly memorize: an octave leap followed by a downward scale:

A clear lead is needed the beat *before* the downward scale starts if everyone is to move off the long note together. If you find this tricky, make the pause a regular number of beats, without saying how many! Beats in brackets should be *felt* but not indicated:

Get everybody to lead, using different lengths of pause. Practice of this will help players to get used to looking up while playing and not just in the gap before a new section starts.

Changes of tempo during a piece also need to be led. A gradual *accelerando* will usually stay together provided everyone is expecting it and listens to what is going on around them. A little encouragement with the eyes from you will probably suffice, along with an indication that the group should start to feel the music in, say, two rather than four beats to the bar if the increase in tempo warrants it. The earlier you can persuade them to feel such a change, the more control you will have. A useful analogy for less experienced players is with changing up a gear when driving. If you leave it too late, the engine will soon be screaming at dangerously high revs.

Similarly, it may help to change down a gear by starting to subdivide beats during a big *rallentando* – indicating quavers instead of crotchets, for example. Novices often find it much harder to slow down than to get faster, especially when excited or nervous, so you may find such passages need extra rehearsal. Try some really exaggerated pull-ups, so that the performance version does not come as a surprise.

A sudden change of tempo in the piece will need at least an upbeat (preferably two beats) at the new speed. This is relatively simple if there is a gap in the music or if, as in much baroque repertoire, the new tempo can be directly related to the old one:

Here, for example, the duple pulse can continue uninterrupted to form a "one in a bar" beat in the triple time section. If no clear relationship can be made, you will have to practise the tricky art of being able to finish a passage in one tempo while anticipating the next. In the next passage you would need to indicate a 2–3 in the new tempo while simultaneously holding the slow semibreve:

It is reassuring to note, however, that after a couple of rehearsals most people can remember specific speeds just as they remember other aspects of the music. Problems seldom arise in performance if you are clear and have rehearsed thoroughly.

One final reminder concerns cut-offs. Chords at the ends of sections (and often elsewhere) will need to finish together. Signal this by a discreet lift or sideways movement of the instrument or head. The quieter the chord, the less flamboyant this gesture should be. As a general tip, you can attract the minutest attention of your ensemble by leaning forward, making the other players feel "gathered" into the group. This is particularly useful for producing really hushed playing, the musical equivalent of a whisper.

The Conductor

Although much of what has been written so far deals specifically with ensembles led by a player, a conductor's rôle covers all of the same ground and more. As well as giving leads and cut-offs, setting tempi and indicating moments where the music is to hold back or surge forward, the conductor is also in a position to hear better than anyone else what is going on. In this way he or she forms a bridge between the players and the audience, and will be the ultimate arbiter on matters of balance, colour and the overall shape of the musical interpretation.

Even the most musically gifted conductor will be of little use to the players without some basic technique. We all know that the movement of a conductor's hand or baton should, at the very least, show the pulse or beat of the music. However, it should also be clear *which* beat, so different time signatures will require slightly different movements. Incidentally, you only need to use one hand for all of this.

The most important beat of any bar is the first, and this is indicated by a **downbeat** vertically in front of the face and upper body. Start the beat at head level to direct the players' attention to your eyes and make sure that the exact impulse of the beat is shown by a clear curve at the bottom, high enough for it to remain in the players' field of vision. Gestures need not be very large – the whole beating pattern should fit within the area of a small TV screen. When working with a new group, it may help to obtain real precision of attack if you hold your left hand as a "ledge" for the curve of the beat to glance off until the players get used to your style.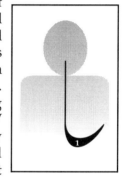

Also remember that these hand movements are meant to guide and reflect the actual flow of the music. Good conductors are aware that music doesn't stop, but merely intensifies, at each pulse, and that the movement of the hand needs to suggest this continuous line. If you conduct like a robot directing traffic, you will get correspondingly jerky playing from your ensemble.

The **upbeat** in any bar should prepare your hand for the next downbeat and will direct the group towards an entry on the first beat of the next bar. It conventionally comes in from your right – all these diagrams are shown from the conductor's view-point: the musicians will see a mirror image of this. Practise the upbeat in the tempo at which you want the music to start.

Beating two in a bar will need a downbeat followed by an upbeat. Make sure that you keep your arm well raised in all these patterns – performers are unlikely to be able to see the focus of the downbeat if it drops to waist level.

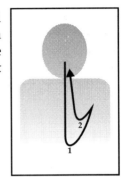

Three time needs an extra beat which you can visualize as glancing across to the right of the imaginary TV screen. Your downbeat will have to incorporate a small loop to the left at the bottom to prepare for this.

Beating in four uses both corners, left then right. Notice that the second beat in four time goes to your left – the opposite direction to the second beat in three time.

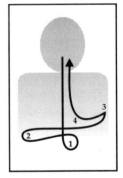

Mastery of these basic patterns will be enormously helpful to your musicians. Try them at different tempi and practise bringing players in on different beats of the bar. As with directing from an instrument, at least two preceding beats will be needed to fix the tempo and allow everyone time to breathe and prepare the entry. It can be helpful to reinforce the actual start point by using both hands. Always look round the group before starting to check that everyone is ready to play and is watching you. With individual leads, don't just wave vaguely in the general direction of a player; instead, direct your gaze and the beat towards them so that, when they look up, you are there for them.

Your beat can communicate not only the tempo but also the mood of the music. It should be possible to show, simply by the way your arm moves, whether you want, for example, a serene, languid 4/4 or a noble, rich 4/4 even though the basic speed remains the same. You will draw much finer *legato* playing from the group if you can keep your hand moving all the time even though, in very slow music, the space between pulses can feel like an age.

Although some conductors do it, there is no need to "mirror" the beat with the other hand. It is far better to use this hand when you want to reinforce something in the score – an instrumental entry, an accented chord or a hushed *pianissimo*, for instance. You can also use it to adjust the balance, signalling for a bit more flute or a lot less trombone, and to indicate cut-offs or final consonants in vocal music.

It would clearly be possible to write a whole book just on conducting – there are several already, if you are interested. Here, however, are just a few more tips. Firstly, get used to conducting with a much lower music stand than you would use when playing – you need to be able to see the musicians and they need to see your beat. Secondly, if you want to beat faster, beat smaller. Gestures often become wilder as musical excitement rises but players will drag behind if faced with a flamboyantly large beat. Finally, don't fall into the trap experienced by many new conductors of beating in time to the music they *hear*. Players always take a moment to respond to your directions and so you will always need to be a fraction ahead of the actual sound. Leading from the front means exactly that – thinking ahead to the next beat, the next bar, the new tempo. Players who have come to expect an instant response from their own instruments find, when conducting, that this extra delay takes some getting used to.

Checklist

◆ **Check** that your directions are clear and can be seen by all

◆ **Practise** setting and changing the tempo,
    giving leads and starting on different beats,
    directing pauses and giving cut-offs

◆ **Remember** that at least two beats are needed to set a tempo
    and remember to *give* the beat, not follow it

Chapter Four

The First Rehearsal

Rehearsal planning

A group which has rehearsed efficiently, with few hold-ups or frustrations, will tend also to perform with greater polish and authority. It may seem obvious, but bitter experience prompts the reminder that confusion over the time or place of a rehearsal will not get your ensemble off to a good start. Make sure that everyone knows about the session well in advance and has brought their instruments and music. See also that there are enough chairs and music stands for everyone and request that players of electric instruments arrive early to set up equipment and check levels – you will learn more about tact and social skills in a few days than would be possible in a year at charm school!

Ideally, it is best to rehearse in the place where the performance will happen. This is often not possible, but try to imagine how you will sit in the concert and stick with this layout in rehearsals. It is important that everyone can see each other and that instruments whose sound is very directional, like the cello, face towards the audience. A semicircle format usually works best, although it may be easiest to put large instruments like piano or double bass at the back.

There are a few other practicalities to bear in mind. Cellists and bassists support their instruments on spikes which need anchoring to the floor to avoid slipping. If spike holders are not used, be prepared to see the spikes used as gigantic gouges to make holes in your venue's precious parquet flooring. Damage of a different kind can result from brass players draining the condensation from their instruments. A school music room floor may well be sufficiently battered for this not to matter, but some offcuts of old carpet may help to avoid anguish over the living-room rugs if you plan to rehearse at home.

Tuning

FOR SALE Three-quarter size violin with bow and hard case. Recently tuned. £45.

It is not hard to see why the small violinist, whose instrument was advertised above, lost interest. Most instruments need tuning every time they are played, with continual adjustment as they warm up or become affected by the temperature and humidity of the surrounding air. These problems are compounded in ensemble playing, with each one needing to be in tune both with itself and with everyone else in the group. Good intonation is one of the hallmarks of a first-rate ensemble, so it is worth devoting considerable care to getting it right.

Although professional musicians often tune to the note A, this is not actually the best tuning note for some instruments: see page 27. If the ensemble contains a fixed-pitch instrument such as piano or organ, whose tuning cannot easily be adjusted, then the group will have to tune to this instrument. Otherwise tuning notes should be given by the instrument with the clearest sound, the pitch having first been checked with a tuning fork. In an orchestra this will usually be done by the oboe, with the strings tuning up first, starting with violins.

It is **essential** that the rest of the players keep quiet while tuning is going on; the sound of someone doing last minute practice will make it impossible for anyone else to tune properly. Long notes at a moderately loud volume will be needed from each player if the pitch is to be assessed accurately. Inexperienced string players should be encouraged to use the full length of the bow for this.

Many string players find it helpful to be given a D minor triad (see upper right) when tuning to the piano, since it allows them to fix the pitches of both their D and A strings. Players may find the strange chord shown lower right even more helpful in highlighting three of the open strings particularly clearly.

Give each player the chance to tune all of their strings to everyone's satisfaction before moving on to the next person. The open strings for the most common instruments are:

Young or inexperienced players may actually ask you to tune their instruments for them. If you also don't feel up to it, see if you can persuade their teacher or a more senior player to help.

Woodwind and brass usually tune next, although they must have had a chance to warm up first. Insist that the strings are quiet, then deal with one instrument at a time. The intonation of wind instruments can vary considerably between notes so it is advisable to check two or three different pitches, generally in the lower-middle range.

Some suggestions for comfortable tuning notes for wind are given opposite – experienced players may have their own preferences. Notes shown in the right-hand column are the pitches actually heard when the player of a transposing instrument sounds the notes on the left. Therefore, if you are giving tuning notes on the piano, you will need to ask for the note in the left-hand column while simultaneously playing its transposed version on the right. For example, you might say "First trumpet, play a G" which you will check against an F on the piano. Most brass, by the way, are best tuned to the tonic, fifth and upper tonic of the key of the instrument. From this you can work out that an E-flat cornet or E-flat tenor horn will need E-flat and B-flat sounding notes (written as C and G), an F tuba (not a transposing instrument) will need F and C, and so forth.

As with the strings, ask wind players to sustain the note until you are sure it is right. A quick toot will not usually be enough. Remember that flaws in the player's technique, such as unsupported breathing or a faulty embouchure, can affect the pitch of notes as much as adjusting the instrument. Watch out for young flautists who let the right arm sag: the flute needs to stay roughly parallel with the floor and the breath must be focused at precisely the right angle to the edge of the mouthpiece if breathy, out-of-tune playing is to be avoided. Horn tuning is affected greatly by the degree to which a player's hand is stuffed into the bell. A few words about an alert posture may help to sort things out if there is a problem.

Written pitches

Sounding pitches (if different)

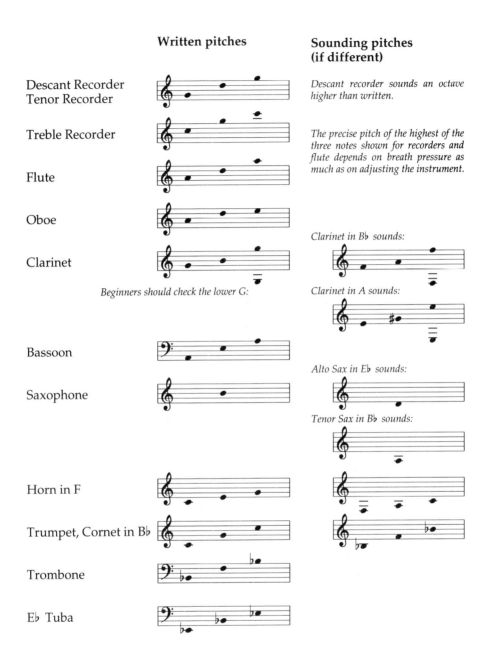

Descant Recorder
Tenor Recorder

Descant recorder sounds an octave higher than written.

Treble Recorder

The precise pitch of the highest of the three notes shown for recorders and flute depends on breath pressure as much as on adjusting the instrument.

Flute

Oboe

Clarinet in B♭ sounds:

Clarinet

Clarinet in A sounds:

Beginners should check the lower G:

Bassoon

Alto Sax in E♭ sounds:

Saxophone

Tenor Sax in B♭ sounds:

Horn in F

Trumpet, Cornet in B♭

Trombone

E♭ Tuba

Unless you are putting together a full orchestra, your group is unlikely to include more than a few of these instruments. If in doubt about how to tune, deal with one instrument at a time, starting with the highest, and don't hurry. Obviously, with experienced players, you should hardly have to intervene at all. Good musicians are already well aware of the importance of accurate tuning and will know that a careful, disciplined approach, even if it takes a few minutes, also helps to settle nerves and focus the concentration of players before the work begins.

Rock bands at this point will also want to spend some time adjusting levels to achieve a satisfactory balance. It is not necessary to rehearse at anything like the volume that you may want to use in the performance – it is easier to hear detail at relatively low levels. Make a note of the setting of each piece of equipment once you are happy with the balance as this will save time at the next meeting.

Other rehearsal preliminaries

Even with a good conductor, and especially if you are working without one, the unanimity of an ensemble depends on musicians listening to each other. Also, eye contact is essential if chords are to start and finish together and you want to look and sound as though you are working as a team. Daring to look up from the music and having to listen outside the individual part on the stand can be scary for players new to ensembles.

It is often worth prefacing the rehearsal proper with some very slow unison scales or a familiar melody that everyone can play without needing the music. If the group includes transposing instruments, remember that these will need to play in a different key to the rest. Persuade everyone to look at each other as they play and concentrate on starting and finishing each note exactly together. Use a variety of volume levels and get different pairs of instruments to play together. Ask them to listen minutely to each other's sound and intonation, and to make adjustments if necessary. This is especially useful with those that operate at different octaves: cello and flute, for example. Try also the exercise for moving off pause notes given in the previous chapter. Vocal groups can be given quite complicated and interesting ensemble exercises – see the chapter on working with voices.

Finally, two small tips which will help to show the other players that you are treating the project seriously and value their support. Firstly, make sure that you know everyone's name (or at very least, their instrument). No one likes to be identified as "You over there behind that big violin-shaped thing". Secondly, bring enough pencils for everyone. You can bet that virtually no one will have brought one, yet you will want them to mark up their parts during the rehearsal. Unfortunately, due to the Disappearing Pencil Syndrome, this will have to be done again at the second rehearsal, and the third. Perhaps you should buy a box wholesale and turn in a tidy profit by selling them on.

Getting started

Once you have tuned and warmed up, it is usually best to jump straight in and try to play the piece through. Every member of the group, having practised the part individually, will be curious to hear how they fit into the ensemble as a whole. If this attempt falls apart (quite likely), don't restart, but try to pick up from the nearest convenient place. Although you will doubtless have already spotted dozens of points that need rehearsing, it will boost everyone's confidence to know that they can get to the end, however sketchily. Remember that there will be other good musicians in the group, aside from you, who will also have noticed their mistakes. They will be able to correct many of these for themselves a second time round.

Get some feedback from the performers about what they think of the piece, how they thought the run-through went and which parts they feel will need special attention. This may also give you some clues, if you need any, of where to start working. Many ensembles conduct all their rehearsals democratically; experienced players will always have much to contribute and, as the group grows familiar with its repertoire and the personalities and skills of its members, less needs to be said and increasingly more becomes intuitive. Other ensembles, however, seem never to be able to agree on anything – a potentially first-rate string quartet once split up before they had even rehearsed together because of arguments over what name to call themselves.

Only you can decide how much democracy your particular group needs. The best advice is to keep your ears open for suggestions while remaining prepared to take decisions if a disagreement requires arbitration. However, if you are preparing the work for a public exam, note that the syllabus may require you to be solely responsible for directing any assessed rehearsals and will not expect you to be helped in this by others.

The beginning is probably as good a place as any to commence the detailed work. Practise starting the piece, making sure that everyone is watching and that your lead or beat is clear. It is worth trying this at different speeds until the group is able to respond accurately and together to any lead you make. Then take just a short section of the music and concentrate on one thing at a time – if you say too much at once the first points you make will have been forgotten by the time the group starts playing.

If you repeatedly hear something strange going on, don't ask who's playing a wrong note as you probably won't get an answer. Instead, reduce the ensemble until you can pinpoint the source – it may simply be a question of someone forgetting to play a sharp or flat. Check that it isn't a printed mistake – a missed accidental in a transposed woodwind part, for instance.

It is a useful technique in many rehearsal situations temporarily to remove instrumental lines from the ensemble in difficult passages. Perhaps ask just the highest and lowest parts to play together. Those playing inner lines will then be able to hear clearly what is going on around them, and you can add their parts back in one at a time, refining and polishing as you go.

Another helpful technique is to make an exercise out of any particularly awkward motif that is shared amongst the group:

Gershwin: I Got Plenty o' Nuttin'

If, for example, bar three is proving troublesome it will save having to repeat the whole phrase if the bar is turned into its own practice routine. This will also make the necessary repetition more fun:

Even at this early stage it is essential to stress to players the importance of dynamic contrasts. You will doubtless already know from playing solo just how much exaggeration, particularly of extreme markings, is needed for an audience to be made aware of changes in dynamics. Having several instruments sounding together, the problem is even more acute; everyone will need to play incredibly softly to produce an effective ensemble *pianissimo*, for example.

Similarly, a group *sforzando* will need extra punch to register with the listeners. It can often be effective to drop the level suddenly before a *crescendo* to strengthen its impact. In a particularly long *crescendo* passage you may need to drop back more than once, giving the illusion of a bigger growth than it is actually possible to make.

Exactly the same care is needed with articulation. Short *staccatos* must be razor-sharp from everyone and rests should be carefully observed – one player can spoil the effect of a silence or muddy someone else's music by holding a note too long.

Suggestions for dealing with more specific ensemble problems appear in later chapters. At the first rehearsal don't try to achieve too much. Players need time to absorb and practise all the things in their parts that the first run-through will have revealed. The next time you meet you'll be amazed how much more confident everyone is. In the meantime, concentrate on carefully polishing just a short section of the music – it will give players an idea of what is required yet also leave them with a sense of achievement at what they have done so far. Plenty of encouragement and praise where due will also boost morale.

Finally, thank the members of your group and fix a time for the next rehearsal. A gap of three or four days will give everyone time to practise but will not allow them to forget what was said. Subsequent rehearsals can be closer together, if necessary, but a week is about the longest gap which is practical if you want to keep a sense of continuity and momentum.

Checklist

◆ **Confirm** time and place of rehearsal well in advance; learn players' names and bring spare pencils

◆ **Tune** carefully, one instrument at a time: not every instrument is best tuned to A. Insist on silence and good posture. Make a note of equipment levels if using amplification

◆ **Warm up** with exercises to encourage the group to watch for leads and to listen to each other

◆ **Run through** the piece first, if possible, noting any repeats then work in detail on the opening section. Concentrate on vivid contrasts and unanimity of ensemble

◆ **Thank** players for their efforts and fix the next rehearsal

Chapter Five

Working with Voices

Elsewhere in this book we have made a lot of assumptions about ensembles. For example, everyone is expected to be able to learn their parts before the first rehearsal and to understand terms like *legato* and *rallentando*. The first thing to remember about vocal groups is that many of their members will know nothing about singing. While you may have some excellent natural voices in your choir, few will ever have practised singing, let alone have a voice teacher, and some may even be hazy about using music notation.

You must therefore expect to spend at least the first few rehearsals teaching notes from scratch (obviously, such preliminary work would not be appropriate for an assessment occasion if your directing forms part of an exam). It will also pay dividends, when you later want to work on shaping and balancing the music, if you have done some work on basic vocal technique with the group.

Unless the rehearsal is very long, don't provide seats for your singers: all singing is best done standing. Get people to stand with their feet comfortably apart and, for warm-up exercises, with arms hanging relaxed at their sides. Remember to keep your gestures high when conducting so the singers don't have to look down; standing on a low platform can help. You may constantly have to remind young singers of the need to keep their teeth apart when singing – although neither should they look as if they are straining to bite into an enormous hamburger.

You can imagine the pitch range of the voice as a ladder. In everyday speech we tend to keep to just the bottom few rungs, using the resonance of the chest to make it audible. Some people try to push this "chest voice" upwards to reach the higher pitches required in singing. Although this is a recognized technique in some types of solo popular music, it seldom allows high notes to be reached and can thus make the inexperienced feel that they cannot sing at all. Higher notes need a smaller resonating space than that provided by the chest – it will help to imagine the sound being formed in the head, almost as if it were being projected from between the eyes. Use of this "head" register will almost certainly be essential to avoid straining for top notes.

Everyone who has worked with vocal groups will probably have come across a "growler" who seems unable to get above the few low pitches used for speaking. Often all that is needed is a little one-to-one help in extending the range, one note at a time. Rather than wrecking someone's confidence for ever by asking them to leave the group, be prepared to offer some individual coaching if you think it may help. After all, they were keen enough to turn up in the first place!

Breathing

Like any wind instrument, the voice will not work properly without controlled, well-supported breathing. Most people take small, shallow breaths when they talk. For singing, however, this will cause poor tone, phrases which fade out and flat intonation. Get the group to practise some controlled deep breathing, perhaps while you count slowly aloud. For example, inhale over a count of three, exhale over a count of five. This exercise should be done standing and ask singers to check that their neck, jaw, shoulder and arm muscles are relaxed as they breathe.

Make sure they are also aware of the ring of muscles underneath the stomach which provide support for the air flow. You can demonstrate how these work with the musical equivalent of a belly laugh:

Ha ha ha ha ha ha, Ha ha ha ha ha.   Ha ha ha ha ha ha, Ha ha ha ha ha.

Try this exercise in different keys with a deep breath beforehand and a really open vowel sound – more like "cat" than "cart". If there are any singers who are uncertain which pitch range is most comfortable for their voice, this will help them to find out. In general the ranges are:

Singing uses much more air flow than talking, and the combination of deep breaths and constant support can be quite physically tiring for those new to it. Getting your group to hum familiar melodies is a very useful way of showing what sort of effort is required without the complications of having to deal with words. To keep everything relaxed, the mouth should be slightly open on an "-ng" sound as in "king". Insist that they breathe only at the ends of phrases and do not slouch forward: bad posture will inhibit the support.

A good, deep breath takes time. Many inexperienced singers don't give themselves a chance because they always breathe too late. Practise bringing the group in, concentrating on this – it often helps if the conductor breathes with the performers. Be generous with your upbeat since a snatched, hurried gesture will provoke a similar response from the singers. Using the left hand can help to make it clear exactly when you want the breath to take place.

Warming up

Try starting the rehearsal with some descending scales, taking care that the semitones, in particular, do not go flat.

Ee - aah, Ee - aah,   Ee - aah, Ee - aah,   Ee - aah, Ee - aah,   Ee - aah, Ee - aah.

Beginning the scale at the top helps to keep the voice "placed" high, well away from the chest register, and should encourage well-focused and clearly projected tone. Starting with "ee" prepares the right shape for a bright "aah", which otherwise can get rather covered and dull on its own. Singers should try not to shape these vowels too much with the lips and teeth. There is no need to form a letter box for each "ee", or a tunnel for "aah" - the difference in sound is made from inside the mouth. Try it yourself while looking in a mirror.

Much vocal music sets several notes to one syllable:

Oo _____ ee _____ aah _____

Take special care with the downward part of this exercise where singers may be tempted to release their support and thus lose control of both pitch and tone. Encourage the group to use the same high-placed voice as in the previous exercise since the chest voice, which many will automatically use for low notes, can become over-extended as the scale rises. Once you are confident that your group can pitch and support scale passages, try an arpeggio exercise:

As well as getting the first 't' together, make sure that no-one sounds the last 't' until *you* give the cut-off at the end – inexperienced singers will want to place the final consonant far too early. As with all the exercises, start this in different keys but remember not to push the altos and basses too high, or the sopranos and tenors too low.

Other useful exercises

Very slow unaccompanied chromatic scales up and down. Check the tuning carefully – semitones are almost always pitched too widely, especially in downward scales.

Give a chord and ask each section to sing a different note of it. Get this in tune and then ask them to move smoothly to a new chord a tone (or semitone) higher or lower.

Take a familiar melody and split the group in two, with half starting on one pitch, and half on another. See how well they can stick to their own parts.

Although the pitch of a sung note is mostly conveyed by the vowel, clear consonants are also essential if your audience is to understand what you are singing about. These should be made at the *front* of the mouth, where possible, so that they can ride on the airflow rather than inhibit it. Check that the final consonants of words are also clear and unanimous. Try singing tongue-twisters on a monotone, such as *Peter Piper picked a peck of pickled pepper,* or the examples overleaf:

Bog - a - bil - la, bog - a - bil - la, Bog - a - bil - la, Bog - a - bil - la, **etc.**

Ral - ler - i - na, Ral - ler - i - na, Ral - ler - i - na, Ral - ler - i - na, **etc.**

The rehearsal

Regardless of whether your eventual performance is unaccompanied, you will need a pitched instrument for the rehearsals (and to give starting notes in the concert) – probably a piano or organ which can play the parts with the singers in the early stages. If you can't play, or want to concentrate fully on directing, remember to fix someone else to act as rehearsal accompanist. Give the person time to prepare the music in advance – playing all the parts of a choral score can be mind-blowingly complicated at times.

Singers may not be used to concentrating with the intensity that you would expect from instrumentalists. You will need to insist, for example, that there is no talking during the rehearsal and that everyone pencils your instructions into their scores. You can help to keep everyone's attention by mixing work on individual parts with music for the whole group to sing. Persuade all singers to listen to what you have to say to one part of the group, as it will almost certainly also apply to the rest as well.

It is probably easiest to teach the notes to one section of the group at a time, possibly at separate rehearsals for each part. Work on just a few bars so there is a chance for the music to sink in – this will also prevent other parts from getting bored sitting around without singing at full rehearsals. Even at this early stage, concentrate on achieving a well-balanced sound from each section, encouraging the timid to sing out while tactfully dissuading others from thinking that it is their solo.

Focus on the words, making sure that consonants are clear and that word endings come when you indicate them. If the sound comes across as muddy or badly blended, check that everyone is using the same bright vowel colours. Special care is needed with **diphthongs** – two adjacent vowel sounds used in some words, for example:

day	*EH - ee*
eye	*AH - ee*
joy	*AW - ee*
loud	*AH - oo*
music	*ee - OO*

These are particularly common in English, and singers must sustain the note on the first vowel, leaving the second until the last moment. With the diphthong in the word "music", however, it is the second sound of the "u" that should be sustained: m*ee - OO* - sic.

Although it is important for the words to be clear to an audience, you will have to decide just how much to make of the consonants. In Latin church music, for instance, it may be equally important to project a seamless musical line; in a number from *West Side Story*, however, clarity of lyrics will be at least as vital as the melody. Watch out particularly for any word that begins with a vowel – singers may easily run a preceding consonant into it and ruin the sense:

Lawlor and Blake: The Sidewalks of New York (bars 1-7)

Remember that you will have to work hard to project sustained, *legato* music in the dry acoustic of many school halls. In a more resonant building, such as a church, this will be much easier – but at the expense of clear words. Bear these factors in mind when you rehearse.

Make sure that the group understands what it is singing about. Have a word-for-word translation ready if the text is in foreign language – many copies will print an English *version* underneath the foreign words, but this will often be only loosely matched to the original. Singers need to know what each particular word on each particular note means if they are to do full justice to the composer's intentions.

Where to breathe

The choice of breathing places is one of the most important aspects of good singing. Insufficient breath will cause problems of flatness and poor tone, and often leads to fragmentary phrasing with little sense of line. Once you have shown the group how to breathe, deeply and relaxed, go through each part marking in breathing places. Clearly, many of these will often be at rests or at punctuation marks in the text. Be prepared to get all singers to cut a long note slightly short if a breath is needed and remember that unanimous breathing can actually increase the rhythmic impact:

Sometimes, however, the music will yield no obvious gaps and the style may demand that singers stagger their breathing. Below is a verse of a well-known Christmas carol with some potential breathing problems. A breath at the end of the first line should work well, but breathing in the middle of the line will make nonsense of the words. If singers cannot sustain the long *Gloria*, staggered breathing during some of the dotted notes will help to disguise the fact from the audience:

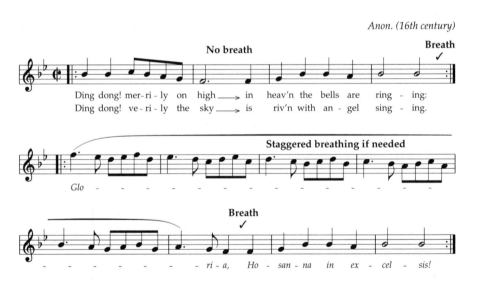

While all singers will need to be reminded to respond early if they are to take a good breath *in*, inexperienced singers may also have to be told to breathe *out*. Although a long sung phrase can feel as if it has drained you of air, in fact you are unlikely to have used even half of your actual reserves. The problem is that what is left is depleted of oxygen and all of it needs to be replaced. If young singers complain of feeling dizzy or faint, this is probably what is happening; some relaxed, full breaths between phrases will generally cure them.

Dynamics and intonation

Most of the features of successful instrumental performance will also apply to singers. Careful attention to dynamic markings is obviously essential, especially bearing in mind that singers may be less confident than other musicians about singing very softly or loudly and will need extra encouragement. Also insist on accurate intonation and check, if there are problems, that everyone is breathing properly and not over-estimating the distance between descending pitches – a common cause of flat singing.

Often you will need to work on sections with a reduced ensemble – say, just sopranos and tenors – so that the out-of-tune part can clearly hear the problem and put it right. If you cannot pinpoint the source of poor intonation immediately, be suspicious of any part which contains the major third of the chord, or which has a leading-note. These are particularly vulnerable pitches for going flat.

Sharp singing is less common, but may occur through forcing a chest voice too high, or if singers push the tone in their anxiety to produce the excitement that you have asked for in the performance. Junior singers may also be prone to shouting if you continually ask for more – greater resonance and clarity are needed more than just sheer lung power.

If, after exploring all these areas, there still seems to be a problem, try transposing the music a semitone higher or lower. Singers often find that F major is, for some reason, a difficult key to tune into – transposition into E or F# may help if the work is unaccompanied. If the pianist cannot cope with such a radical solution, suggest instead that they play an octave higher than written. If using an organ, avoid dull-toned stops and stick to bright timbres. All these techniques can help to pull the intonation into shape.

You will be able to improve the tuning, tone and appearance of the group if you encourage singers to smile (even if only with their eyes). Remember that choirs, like instrumental ensembles, will respond to your mood and will enjoy themselves if *you* seem to be having fun – they will sound dull and reticent if you are nervous or bad tempered.

Finally, don't be afraid to put reinforcements from another part onto a weak or dodgy lead if it will help boost the attack and singers' confidence. High tenor parts can often be much improved with the help of a few strong altos, for example. Similarly, consider using just solo voices or a small semi-chorus on any section which seems to require more delicacy than you can achieve with the full ensemble.

Presentation

As has been mentioned elsewhere, audiences have eyes as well as ears and nothing looks worse than an ill-assorted group, unclear where and how to stand. You will find more about preparation for the actual performance in the final chapter. In the meantime make sure that copies, if they are used, are held with two hands, and high enough for singers to be able to see both the music and your beat without having to move their heads. It may be worth providing folders if the group is singing several different pieces – you can be sure otherwise that someone will drop something during the performance.

Insist that page turns are made noiselessly - obviously everyone will turn at virtually the same moment and the cumulative rustle can be quite distracting. If the group is singing from memory, you will have to decide what singers are to do with their hands. The best solution is for them to hang loosely at the sides; however with young, fidgety singers, it may be easier to have them lightly clasped behind the back – a position which also allows a good, open posture for singing.

Checklist

◆ **Begin** with breathing and warm-up exercises for good placing of the voice, resonant tone and secure intonation

◆ **Rehearse** with the singers standing up, aim for good discipline and ensure that your points about breathing, dynamics, and so forth, are pencilled into copies

◆ **Listen out** for accurate intonation (particularly on repeated notes, semitones and other danger spots), clear diction, unanimous final consonants and pure, open vowels

Chapter Six

Jazz and Pop

Almost everything in the previous chapters of this book can be applied to music in just about any style. The techniques of producing and communicating musical ideas require the same discipline, polish and imagination, regardless of whether you are playing Bach or Blues Brothers. However, there are some additional skills needed by the director of a rock or jazz group if rehearsals and performances are to run smoothly and productively.

The Routine

Unless you have a set of fully notated parts, the group will probably be playing from an outline score, such as a "lead sheet", or perhaps even from just chord symbols (either written out or memorized). In order to construct a complete piece from this you will need to work out a "routine" in advance and give each member of the band a copy. This might consist of instructions such as:

◆ Intro:	4 bars	Piano and drums (2 bars)
		Bass guitar bridge (solo for 2 bars)
◆ Verse 1:	8 bars	Lead guitar solo
		Accompanied by piano, bass and drums
◆ Chorus:	8 bars	Tutti (with walking bass)
		Lead guitar and trumpet in 3rds
◆ Verse 2:	8 bars	Trumpet solo with lead guitar fills
		Accompanied by bass and drums only
◆ Chorus:	8 bars	As before
	2 bars	Drum fill
	8 bars	Repeat chorus, semitone higher
◆ Outro:	2 bars	Last 2 bars of chorus; repeat to fade

Before the first rehearsal you will need to find out from your players whether a lead sheet with a routine is sufficient. Remember that instruments such as trumpet, clarinet and sax will need suitably transposed copies of the notation unless the players can transpose fluently at sight. Make sure everyone understands precisely what the chord symbols mean. For example, the figure 7 by itself always refers to a minor seventh, so **C⁷** means a chord of C plus B flat, while **Cᵐᵃʲ·⁷** means a chord of C plus B natural. A useful tip, if the work is largely improvisatory, is to write out the chord symbols separately. Many musicians find it easier to invent new material on a bare harmonic framework than to see the chords fleshed out with a melody, which may limit the flow of their ideas.

In order to avoid wasting time, have a clear idea in advance of the rôle for each instrument throughout the piece. So, if a backing for trumpet and sax is not already written out, decide on some simple instruction such as "trumpet take the fifths of the chords, sax take the thirds and leave the roots for the bass". The way to end the piece may also need your attention: the fade-outs so popular in recording don't work nearly so well live, so you may have to devise a coda to provide a clear finish. Warn players to damp any instrumental resonance on the last note if you want a really slick ending – nothing sounds worse than a crash cymbal or open guitar string ringing on after everyone else has stopped.

You should also have a clear idea of the style you want from the group. This may involve writing out in advance some key features, such as brass stabs to accompany a guitar improvisation, a guide bar or two to show the type of keyboard pattern you want, or perhaps an important drum fill. You may have a bassist who can play from chord symbols, but he or she will need to know if you want the style to be reggae, disco, slow ballad, jazz funk, walking bass, eighths, or whatever. Note that many jazz players will automatically "swing" quavers which rock musicians would play straight. Make sure that everyone knows what you want.

The rehearsal process

Most pop and jazz will include some degree of improvisation and this takes time to develop – plenty of warming-up and playing-in will help get the best from the musicians. However, it is important that the rest of the group are not kept waiting around while one player tries to perfect a solo that might better be done in a separate session with just a pianist. Solos can be roughly sketched in at early rehearsals, so that you can concentrate on the blend, balance and refinement of the group as a whole.

You may well find that the musicians produce a wealth of individual ideas which don't coalesce too well. It will be your job to describe or identify the effect you want, and encourage the members of the group to copy and develop it. You may need, for example, to ask the bass player to reserve some brilliant passagework for a later solo and to provide a less cluttered part that won't muddy the complex texture currently being rehearsed. Or perhaps the drummer and bass player will need to listen to each other separately so that kick drum notes can support the accents of the bass part rather than cutting across them.

Players will certainly need a clear idea of how to treat *tutti* sections. Do you expect a smooth, chord-based texture to accompany a singer in the chorus, or do you want a counterpoint of improvised melodic lines more in the style of traditional jazz? If chords, are they to be held as sustained semibreves or do you want a rhythmic pattern? Experiment during rehearsal should be encouraged, but early decisions on all such fundamental matters will allow time for improving the performance rather than continually changing it. If in doubt, always keep things simple and elegant.

Less experienced groups can be tempted to tackle too much in a rehearsal – perhaps getting one song just about together before going on to try some new cover version or enjoying a general jam session. As with all ensemble playing, get your band used to the idea that "getting it together" is just the first stage in the rehearsal process. If you are playing in the band, make sure that you get a chance to listen in detail to the total sound. This will almost certainly mean listening from some distance away, particularly when amplification is used.

Amplified instruments

We have already mentioned the importance of getting guitarists, synth players and anyone else using amplification to set up well before the start of the rehearsal. You will need to check that key players can hear one another. This may require, for example, the use of floor monitors for the drummer to hear the bassist, and for a singer to hear the synth.

Once equipment is positioned and connected, and the players have warmed-up and tuned, you will need to carry out a balance test. If the group includes more than just a couple of amplified instruments it is advisable to have an additional person to act as engineer and to take notes of preferred settings. You, as director, should nevertheless make the final decisions about all matters of balance – not just the relative volume levels of each instrument, but also their stereo positioning, the use of EQ (affecting brightness of tone, and so forth) and any effects that are being used. You may, for example, decide that some reverb is needed on the synth and vocals, but not on the guitars or drums.

As a rule, players new to group work will seriously over-estimate how loud to set their instruments. There is a great temptation for each musician to keep nudging up his or her volume in order to be heard: be prepared to be ruthless in keeping levels realistic. Less experienced players may also be annoyingly keen to demonstrate every sound on their synth or every guitar effect. Of course, some experimentation will be needed in rehearsal, but it will save time if you go through the individual parts in advance, deciding with the keyboardist which patches to program and helping guitarists with the effects and playing styles that they will need.

Remember that rehearsing at reduced levels will help you to hear what is going on and will encourage, particularly from guitarists, exploration of more subtle techniques which may well enhance the work. The final performance of pop music is, however, sometimes quite different from its rehearsal. If you are to perform at a large gig with lighting and stage effects, you will need to rehearse at the actual venue, checking stage movements (particularly to ensure the guitar leads don't get tangled), performing with intense lighting, wearing the clothes you have chosen for the event, and playing at full levels. Even here, though, care needs to be taken to get the *musical* effect you want. A bass guitar played over a stack of monitors with maximum low frequency gain may sound wonderful from several streets away, but in the hall itself such extreme bass tip-up may result in a fuzzy, un-focused rumble that simply masks the efforts of everyone else.

Microphone technique

Unless you are lucky enough to be able to draw on the services of an experienced vocalist, you should be prepared to solve problems of microphone technique for any singers in the group. Here is a brief checklist of just some of the things that can occur which may require your help:

Singing too close to the mike. Turn **up** the level of the vocals: this should frighten the singer enough to correct the problem.

Too much contrast between louds and softs. The easiest solution is an electronic one: compress the signal to reduce the dynamic range.

Fading due to varying the distance between mike and mouth. A mike on a stand may be better than a hand-held mike. Position singers with backs against a wall if they cannot resist moving around.

Dull vocal tone. Boost EQ around 3 to 5 kHz. Try to reduce this low treble range on accompanying instruments.

Thin vocal tone. Doubling-up singers on the part may help, as may applying effects such as chorusing or a very short delay to the signal. If other members of the group are going to join in on sections of the vocal, remember that they will also need mikes and stands.

Feedback or howlround. The intense scream caused by the singer's mike picking up the amplified signal from the monitor and sending it back for yet more amplification. The use of a unidirectional mike should help a lot – one with a cardioid response pattern will reject most signals from unwanted directions. Position the singer to the side of the monitors, not in front of them.

Excessive pop on the plosives P and B. Use a shield made from a piece of some old tights, stretched on a wire coathanger, in front of the mike. For live performance, a foam "pop shield" over the mike will look better, although these do tend to reduce high frequencies.

Excessive hiss on sibilants such as S and T. Use a low-quality dynamic mike with limited high-frequency response. Try to get the vocalist to sing across the mike, not into it.

Excessive breath noise. Suspend the mike on a boom, pointing down towards the floor.

Difficulty in synchronizing rhythm and/or pitch with the band. There can be several reasons for this. The vocalist may simply be unable to hear their own singing – in which case provide an extra floor monitor (or headphones, if recording) and use this system to relay the microphone signal back to the singer, preferably with some reverb. If the vocalist cannot hear some critical element in the accompaniment, such as the bass or keyboard, the same can be done with a signal relayed from these instruments. Another cause may be inability to hold the correct rhythm or pitch in the middle of a complex texture. A guide part played on a spare synth (or a guide track, if recording) and again routed to just the singer may help. Finally, there may of course be problems with the singer's technique, such as insufficient breath support resulting in flatness. The chapter on working with voices gives some suggestions for dealing with this.

Finally, take every opportunity to record the group in action. Even a portable cassette recorder will give you vital information about balance, ensemble and technique which is easy to miss when playing. If you can get hold of a video camera, you can check that the band looks OK as well.

Checklist

◆ **Prepare** the routine, if needed, in advance. Make sure you know what each player is expected to do, especially in *tutti* sections. Know the style you are aiming for.

◆ **Encourage** exchange of ideas in rehearsal, but make firm decisions. Keep the goal of the rehearsal in view, and discourage unproductive fiddling with gadgetry.

◆ **Be aware** of the techniques you may need in dealing with microphones and amplified instruments.

Chapter Seven

Creating an Interpretation

Once everyone has learnt their parts and can come in at the right places, respond to dynamic and articulation markings and be alert to your direction, the really creative aspect of rehearsing can begin.

The director's job is partly a matter of co-ordination and partly about communication. Ask yourself what an audience requires from a musical performance. It is entitled to expect:

◆ Right notes with good intonation

◆ Clear words

◆ Unanimous, well-balanced ensemble

◆ A group which has taken the trouble to look good on stage

You, as co-ordinator, will have made sure that all these things are present in the performance as a matter of courtesy to the audience and self-respect for the musicians. However, your listeners will be much more excited if they also get:

◆ Music which is rhythmically alive

◆ Phrasing that is expressive and always has shape and direction

◆ An interpretation which creates a real sense of atmosphere

◆ Performers who are totally absorbed in what they are doing and who seem to be enjoying themselves

Of course, these lists are not really separate at all; most of what is contained in the second will be made possible by the thoroughness with which you deal with the points raised in the first. There is an old saying that genius is 1% inspiration and 99% perspiration. Paradoxically, it will be the groups that have worked hardest and in the greatest detail which will sound freshest and most spontaneously expressive in performance.

Rhythmic vitality

For the music to sound rhythmically alive, you will first need to be clear what beat you want everyone to feel. If a section seems sluggish and lacks bounce, try it with fewer pulses in the bar – two instead of four, for instance. In slow music, it may help for the group to take a section much faster than usual until they get the feel of this longer pulse. Slow it back to normal but ask the ensemble to remember what it felt like at the quicker speed. If it is dance music, would the way they are playing persuade people to get to their feet?

Make sure that everyone is observing printed articulation marks – slurs and staccatos, for example, along with any accents that appear. Often there will be no detailed instructions printed in the parts and you will be expected to work out your own. In many baroque continuo parts, for instance, a quaver bass line written as shown left can enliven the music hugely if it is played as shown right:

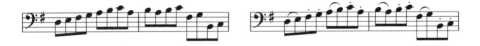

Printed note lengths are only ever a guide to performers, and rhythms can often be sharpened up by judicious insertion of a short rest:

More radical alteration of rhythm for rehearsal purposes can also help to shed light on apparently uninteresting passagework. Try, for example, persuading your group to "swing" pairs of even notes in baroque music. For some reason, this highlights all the joyfully dizzy invention while banishing any rhythmic monotony. When you restore the straight version it should take on a totally new feel.

Check that everyone is clear about what you want. A passage such as:

will sound blurred if even one player is ignoring the *staccatos*. You, as director, should notice that no articulation is shown in the cello part, so the cellist will probably need to be told to match the articulation of the two flutes in bar three.

In vocal or instrumental counterpoint, where similar music occurs in different parts at different times, unanimity of articulation will help to clarify the structure for the listener:

It may be useful to get everyone in the quartet to play the first bar of their lead simultaneously, in octaves, to standardize the articulation. Try this several times then, when you play it staggered, each part should know how to imitate the preceding one. As each part enters, it will also help if those already playing drop back in dynamic to make room for the new entry to be heard. You can see that this is particularly important for the second violin lead, which is not only competing with three other parts but which also delightfully enters two beats earlier than expected. Your interpretation will make a much greater impact if such points are communicated effectively to the audience.

Sometimes, fuzzy ensemble can be cured simply by checking that players with similar parts are listening to each other. For example, this music is unlikely ever to be completely together if the violin tries to fit with the oboe while the viola is listening only to the cello:

Mozart: Oboe Quartet, K.370 (first movement: bars 46-48)

Similarly, you may be able to tighten up a bass guitar part by making sure that the bassist is listening to the drummer rather than the singer. Drummers, of course, have never been known to listen to anybody!

Another useful tip for obtaining cohesive rhythm: performers often find it difficult to move off some tied notes early enough. This is particularly problematic in fast-moving contrapuntal music where there is little room for flexibility:

Bach: Cantata No.51 (Jauchzet Gott in allen Landen: bars 25-27)

Practise first omitting the tie, so that each of the semiquavers is in the right place. Next, encourage the musicians to feel the impulse of the tied note without actually playing it – possibly by leaving a semi-quaver rest. There is then time to breathe, re-position the bow, etc., before moving off again. Alternatively, if a gap is not wanted, try a *crescendo* through the long note, aiming its focus on the tied note.

If you are working on a baroque piece, you should be aware of the performance conventions of the time. These are not just matters of interest to the musicologist but interpretative decisions that will bring the music to life, as shown by the success of the many "authentic" recordings of recent years. This is not the place for a full account of performance practice, but it is worth noting that many of the conventions arose because the notation did not always give an exact account of the precise rhythms and decorations to be applied in performance – rather like more recent jazz and pop scores. For example, dotted rhythms usually need to match the main rhythm patterns of the movement. This may mean treating the uppermost pattern shown right as essentially a triplet rhythm. In other cases, the pattern may need to be treated as a double dotted rhythm if demi-semiquavers form a predominant feature of the music.

Most baroque music needs lively articulation – string players often talk of playing "off the string", allowing the bow to leave the string between notes. You may wish to encourage players to use vibrato primarily as an ornament, rather than as a continuous feature of the sound, and to persuade keyboard players to consider adapting editors' realizations of continuo parts where necessary. You will certainly need to insist on unanimous rhythm in ornaments (both notated and improvised), to emphasize rhythmic dislocations such as the hemiola, and to encourage performers to elaborate their printed parts on repeats and in any place suitable for a cadenza.

Phrasing and balance

Phrasing is about highlighting the melodic architecture of music. For singers and wind players it is inextricably bound up with breathing; for strings it concerns the bow. Other instrumentalists can improve immeasurably the way that they shape a melody by thinking of how they would sing it. You will probably have heard performances in which the music seems to flow effortlessly and yet the player or singer still has all the time in the world to breathe or start afresh. Every note seems to be in exactly the right place with precisely the right colour and volume. In short, the music sounds irresistibly right.

Good musicians know, often instinctively, that each melodic phrase has a point which notes either lead towards or fall back from. You can think of it as being shaped like an arch, although the apex is often nearer the end of the phrase than in the middle, and there may be several such arches in long phrases. Frequently there will be no indication printed in the part of where the phrase is leading – no *crescendo* or *diminuendo* – yet, by subtle heightening of momentum and colour, the phrase's internal architecture can be brought out:

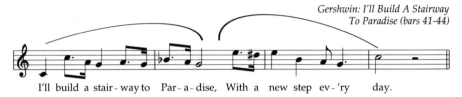

Gershwin: I'll Build A Stairway
To Paradise (bars 41-44)

I'll build a stair-way to Par-a-dise, With a new step ev-'ry day.

In ensemble music two or more instruments will often share important material in dialogue with one another:

Mozart: String Quartet in D, K.499 (first movement: bars 66-69)

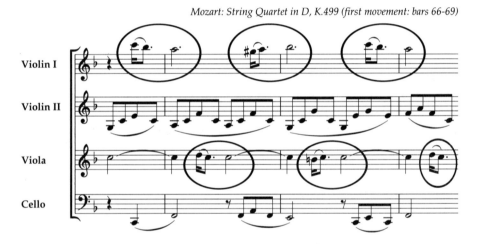

Help your players discover which of their music is melodic and which is accompaniment and get them to play sections to the others. Discuss where the highpoint of each phrase might be and compare notes with players who have similar passages. Once you have discovered who has the melody in a section, get those with accompanying material to follow the shape of the melodic phrase, listening and responding to the part with the tune. This will hugely increase the expressive power of the performance and the new flexibility will liberate the melody to be phrased even more elegantly. Adjust individual levels until the melody is sufficiently prominent to draw the listener's attention while the accompaniment is nicely balanced within itself.

Balance needs particular care when trying to highlight instruments which are playing in soft parts of their register, such as low flutes, or those which might be masked by louder instruments in the ensemble.

Some players are very reticent about taking a solo part. You may have heard one of the countless jokes about viola players – *How do you get violists to play sixty-four perfectly even hemidemisemiquavers? Give them a semibreve and write "solo" over it.* In fact, most viola players love solos providing they are confident they will be heard.

Another instrument that needs sensitive balancing is the piano, whose tonal power can be overwhelming in smaller ensembles. It is, for example, all too easy for a pianist to obliterate the cello's tenor range. With a grand piano, you will need to decide whether you want the lid fully open, on "half-stick" or closed completely. Remember, when positioning the group, that most of the sound of an upright piano is projected from the back of the instrument. Saxophones have a tendency to mask almost everything except other saxophones in small ensembles, and those keen to encourage the brass to play out should note the advice of Sir Thomas Beecham to student conductors: "never, never look a trombonist in the eye".

In the end, successful balance will depend on your knowledge of the music and careful listening to the players or singers that you have. Always get an opinion from further back in the hall – acoustics on stage can be notoriously unrepresentative – and you need to know what the audience will hear.

Atmosphere and commitment

Creating a sense of atmosphere with your performance depends on several factors. At the most basic level, the group needs to decide on what it is they wish to **communicate** in their performance. Hopefully, this will include a love of the music, a sense of creative co-operation and a feeling of inner energy and confidence.

Effective communication will also depend on agreement about the mood of the music. Sometimes this will be suggested by a title, such as "Nocturne", or by a performing direction like *con fuoco*. Often, though, the mood will not be so explicit. You may decide that the essence of a baroque "Allegro" is in the excitement of its driving motor rhythms or that the focus of a fugue should be the clarity and energy of the individual lines. The function of the music will also dictate its mood – is it a religious piece, for example, a dance or a piece of nightclub sleaze? A successful performance will reflect an intellectual response to the music as well as an instinctive emotional one. You may decide, for example, that the essential thing to communicate in a classical sonata movement is the elegance and balance of the phrasing, the logic and shape of its formal design.

With less experienced musicians, it may help to try and find words which describe the mood you wish to communicate. The more precise you can be, the better the chance that you will be understood. Therefore, rather than "happy" try:

◆ boisterous, cheerful, contented, humorous or frivolous.

Focus in on the word "sad" and try to discover whether the music is:

◆ tragic, doom-laden, angry, wistful, nostalgic or solemn.

Is the music elegantly stylized, dramatic, aggressive, laid back, dreamy or distracted? You may feel that this is hopelessly simplistic – after all music cannot adequately be described in words. However, you may also be surprised just how much discussion will be needed before players will agree on even these simple adjectives. The mere fact that you are exploring the topic will help to provoke the group into thinking about the expressive content of what they present.

Instrumentalists and singers will continually need to be reminded that music is fundamentally a means of communication. Expressive playing or singing must have something to express, even if you can't find words to describe what it is. The more the group can share a common purpose in trying to communicate this to an audience, the better the performance will be.

Effective rehearsing of a piece of music will gradually build a kind of mental commentary which runs alongside the notes in each person's part. Every bar or section will have attached to it points for the performer to remember about individual technique, breathing places, dynamics, colour, tempo, ensemble and mood, all of which will have come up in rehearsal or practice sessions. Most of these points should be written into the parts as they arise, otherwise you will have to cover much of the same ground next time.

The mood component of this commentary may, as in the case of a song, be influenced by an actual story, or it may be much less tangible: a mixture of odd words, images and feelings which only make sense when you play – the glittering ballroom of a minuet or the moonlit night of a nocturne. Even within the same group, players will actually find different ways of expressing these ideas: sharing them will help everyone to express the mood of the music unanimously.

In rehearsal, get everyone used to the idea of having emotional as well as technical "signposts". These will help the group to recall how the music should feel each time they perform it and will also give people something to hold onto if they feel nervous or distracted on the day. It often helps to pin down the mood of slightly difficult or ambiguous music if you ask the group to imagine that it is the soundtrack of a film or video, and then get them to visualize the images on screen that it might accompany. Young players are often particularly good at this, and the sophistication of their imagery can be quite startling.

When preparing your interpretation, remember that your listeners have eyes as well as ears: they will notice if a performer looks bored or uncomfortable and they will be confused if a slow, sad piece ends with a sudden grand flourish of instruments or if, after something with real panache, the group looks dejected and miserable. Persuade your musicians that, in order to communicate fully, they need to project not only the music, but also their own enjoyment and excitement in performing it. All too often a player's criterion for a satisfactory performance is one in which nothing goes wrong. Audiences will trade any number of mistakes for a spark of excitement from the platform to show their presence is important and appreciated.

Checklist

◆ **Work on articulation** to achieve rhythmic vitality and, where required, unanimous attack. Listen out for problems with dotted rhythms and tied notes.

◆ **Shape phrasing** to highlight the musical line.

◆ **Balance** each part to make the structure of the music clear and to avoid important parts of the texture being masked.

◆ **Find the focus of the music** by discussing its mood and purpose. Explore the group's intellectual and emotional responses to the piece and help them to find ways of communicating these to the audience.

Chapter Eight

Working In Detail

Most of this book deals with general techniques for rehearsing and performing ensemble music. The repertoire is so large and so varied that it would be impossible to give detailed help for every type of piece and, after all, each group will encounter its own individual problems. You, the director, will have to identify and focus on the particular points that need attention.

Those who have ever attended a masterclass, or had professional coaching, will already know just how much attention to detail is needed if you want to produce really polished playing or singing. There simply are no shortcuts. Ensembles performing live will always sound ragged if the rehearsing has been sketchy. Bands who go into the recording studio unprepared, relying on the engineers to tidy up the tracks afterwards, would save a fortune on studio time by sorting out the detail beforehand. In this chapter are two examples to give you a flavour of the sort of detailed work you must expect to do with your group if you want the best possible results.

The following extract is from a trio for clarinet, viola and piano:

Mozart: Trio in B♭ , K.498 (Minuet: bars 1-4)

There is no tempo marking, but *The New Grove Dictionary of Music and Musicians* describes the minuet as "an aristocratic social dance ... dignified, graceful, relaxed and unaffected". This may lead you to a moderately slow, elegant tempo.

Decide how long you want the crotchets to be in the piano left hand and viola parts. The absence of slurs often means that notes can be slightly detached – this will help the dance feel. It is possible that a young pianist may not have a wide enough hand span to manage the octaves. If this is the case, should they play upper or lower notes?

Notice that the clarinet part is printed as the player will see it and must therefore be read a tone lower for concert pitch. It is actually in unison with the top of the piano part. Check that tuning and articulation are exactly matched, with all three instruments unanimous in bar four. Remember that the clarinet will need room to breathe at the end of this bar. The curved lines are slurs, not phrase marks, so no breath should be taken before this point. Indeed, all three players should ensure that the four-bar section is treated as a single unit, setting up a pattern of regular phrasing that is such an important part of dance music.

Where pairs of notes are slurred together in classical music, the second note is usually played lighter than the first. Compare the two slurred notes on clarinet and piano in bar three with the ones in bar four. Decide which pair should drop away most and make sure that everyone is doing the same amount.

Discuss where the focus of the four-bar phrase should be. There is an early point of tension at the start of bar two, where the D is tied across the barline to produce a suspension. The piano will inevitably die away on this note, but the clarinet can make the point with a crescendo through bar one – this will probably mean starting a little below the *forte* shown in the score.

You will probably all agree that bar two could use a slight increase in momentum to carry the four-bar phrase forward. If you decide that the impetus of the phrase continues into the first beat of bar four, the viola, in particular, will need to carry the intensity through bar three as well, pulling the clarinet and piano with it. It may help to highlight the shape further if you think of the pulse as a very slow one to the bar, rather than the three beats suggested by the time signature.

Really good players will deal with most of these points intuitively as well as being able to produce the heightened sense of shape and colour needed for the concert platform. Unless the group is really experienced, however, you will almost certainly have to work at many of these areas consciously so that everyone knows not only how to play their part but also what to listen for from the others.

The next extract is from an *a cappella* setting of a Grace for four-part choir:

Charles Wood: Oculi Omnium (bars 1-7)

The entries of the four parts are not just imitative – the whole piece is a canon. However, when you prepare the score you should notice that it is a rather ingenious canon. The sopranos and altos begin by descending a major triad but, because of their starting pitches, the tenors descend a diminished triad while the basses sing down a minor triad. If you are working with inexperienced singers you may find it quicker to teach basic notes to each part of the choir in separate sectional rehearsals, so that the two lower parts are not misled by the subtly different soprano and alto parts. However, notice that each part enters on the same note that the previous part has just reached. This will need some careful listening in full rehearsal so that there are no differences in intonation between the parts and that no bumps in volume are caused when different parts coincide on the same note.

The words are in Latin and mean "The eyes of all wait upon You, Lord". The word *Te* (pronounced "tay" and meaning "You" – i.e. God) is the focus of the phrase and, ideally, this first long phrase should be taken in one breath to preserve the meaning of the words.

Singers will be tempted to breathe after the first three descending notes, since the next note rises. Try to get them to sing the phrase in a single breath, with a *crescendo* through *Te* – both to mark the climax and to fix the tied-note rhythm in that bar. Encourage a soft start, despite the fairly high first note, in order to allow room for later growth. Less experienced singers may find a *crescendo* towards the end of a long phrase is too much to cope with in one breath – try staggered breathing if there is a risk of *Te* going flat (it is the difficult major 3rd of a triad for both sopranos and altos).

Singers will have to breathe early because the passage starts with a vowel, which needs a moment's more preparation than a consonant. However, make sure that they do not anticipate the 'c' in *oculi* (think of it as *o-cu-li*). The second vowel needs a pure "oo" – singers may need to be coaxed away from a very English *oc-yoo-lee* pronunciation. The final 't' of *sperant* can go neatly on the first beat of the rest in the following bar, still leaving space to breathe for the next phrase. Emphasise the consonant 'D' of *Domine* in bar seven (imitated by the lower voices in succeeding bars) since this is both a significant word in the text and also an entry in an unexpected part of the bar (the second beat) which will add musical interest to the performance.

Both of the examples in this chapter are concerned with only the opening few bars of music of much longer pieces. You will need, by careful analysis, to make similar decisions about the function of every note in the piece you are working on, and how it should therefore be presented in performance.

Checklist

◆ **Analyse** the music you are preparing, in order to decide:

◆ The **focal point** of each phrase and of the piece as a whole

◆ The **rôle and relative balance** of each part in contributing to that focal point

◆ **Devise ways** to communicate to performers your idea of the purpose and direction of the music, and be ready to suggest the technical means by which your goals can be achieved

Chapter Nine

The Performance

No amount of rehearsing can quite prepare you for the difference that having an audience will make. Provided the group feels confident that it knows the music and understands exactly how you want it, the extra excitement will usually generate even better playing or singing than expected. As director, however, you will know that really slick presentation needs careful attention to detail outside the performance of the music itself. Here are a number of things you can do in advance to ensure that your musicians are able to perform at their best, and that both they and the audience enjoy themselves on the day.

◆ Practise walking on and off stage – with singers it is particularly important that everyone goes on in a pre-determined order otherwise people may find themselves standing in the wrong place. Firmly discourage members of the group from waving to friends and relations from the stage as it won't help in creating the sense of drama that you need to surround the performance.

◆ Decide what everyone should wear. From the audience's point of view it is important that you look good as well as sound good.

◆ If there are to be programmes, write some notes about the music and players which will help to set the scene for the audience. Don't be afraid to express your personal view of the music – readers will certainly find this more interesting than, say, the composer's place of birth. Otherwise prepare a few words of introduction which you can use after the group has tuned up. Memorize this beforehand – as far as the audience is concerned it is part of the performance.

◆ Discuss how the group is to acknowledge applause both before and after the music. Groups without a conductor will normally all bow together once before sitting down to tune and will bow at least once more at the end before walking off. Practise getting the bows poised and synchronized, with everyone following your lead. Nervous or inexperienced players may be tempted to rush through this aspect of performing – remind them that the audience needs plenty of time to show its appreciation and that a hurried nod from the stage will risk appearing clumsy or even downright rude.

◆ If you are conducting, it is usual to take the bows yourself and acknowledge the players' contribution at the end. In this case the ensemble will need to practise walking off after you have left the stage. If there is applause during the piece, or between movements, suppress your irritation that some jerk in the audience doesn't realise that you haven't yet reached the end; instead, accept the compliment that someone out there is really enjoying themselves.

◆ Make sure that you have arranged for chairs and music stands to be set out before the group comes on. The person responsible for this will need to be briefed well in advance about the exact layout that you want; what music goes on which stand; whether you are conducting from a podium; how you want the lid of the piano and whether a chair is needed for the pianist's page turner. Check that someone *has* been asked to turn pages for the pianist if need be.

◆ Find out if there is a room for players to leave coats and cases, and whether it is out of earshot of the hall, so that it can be used for warming up before the performance.

◆ Well before the day of the show, reassure yourself that there is adequate lighting for the group to play by – it may be too late to get more in by the time you come to rehearse on the day. The final rehearsal should be undertaken with full lighting so that players can check that they are neither dazzled nor in shadow. Bands will need a specific lighting rehearsal if light effects form a significant part of the gig. Check in any case that there are enough power sockets for your equipment and that your leads are long enough to reach them.

Reading through these points you will probably feel that most of them are just common sense. However, as the excitement builds in the days leading up to the performance, it can be all to easy to forget these simple details. Remember that your players will probably be nervous enough on the day without having to cope with organizational hiccups which could, with forethought, have been avoided. Insist that the group treats all the details of presentation as seriously as they do the actual playing. Have plenty of run-throughs of the whole performance, including bowing and walking on and off. Record yourselves if possible – the presence of a running tape recorder is a good substitute in rehearsal for the adrenaline created by an audience. Better still, video a rehearsal so that everyone can actually see how they appear. One violinist was completely disbelieving when told that he was in the habit of absent-mindedly picking his nose with the point of his bow, until he was shown the filmed evidence.

On the day itself, present a calm and confident exterior to your players, regardless of the nervous turmoil and panic that you may be feeling inside. Organise a short rehearsal in the hall, leaving plenty of time afterwards before you are due to perform. If the venue is some distance away, remind players to allow ample time for the journey – one late arrival will unsettle everyone else.

It is important that this final rehearsal does not end up demoralizing everybody. It is too late to make any drastic changes, so try instead to be encouraging and to infect the group with you enthusiasm (even if you have to fake it!). Professional musicians will often use this session merely to "top and tail" the music, reminding themselves of tempi, testing the balance and rehearsing the start and finish. There is no need to go over and over the piece blunting everyone's appetite for the performance. It is far better just to get the group comfortable and focused and then trust to the excitement of the occasion in generating its own momentum for later.

Remind everybody to be back in good time for the concert. You may need to organise something to prevent excited younger performers from rushing around and tiring themselves out. A quiet room and a pile of comics will help to keep them calm. Try to prevent singers eating crisps or chocolate before they go on, as these will not help the voice. Once you do finally get on stage, take plenty of time over tuning and getting settled, both for your own comfort and to allow the listeners to get on your wavelength.

It can often be difficult for performers to remember what it is like to be in the audience. While you are possibly nervous and buzzing with a hundred different thoughts about the details of the performance, the audience is likely to be relaxed and looking forward to an enjoyable show. From their point of view, a successful performance is one that allows them to feel confident that you are in control so that they can simply sit back and let the music happen. If you have done your job properly, most of the audience will probably not even be conscious of all the hard work that has gone into preparing the entertainment. They will be generously forgiving (or more likely oblivious) of mistakes – after all, most will know that they couldn't get up there and play themselves – and they will be delighted to feel that your performance has got through to them. Music is about sharing, and your efforts will, for a brief moment, enable your listeners to be musicians too.

Index